William Griggs, Bernard Quaritch

Facsimiles of Illustrations in Biblical and Liturgical Manuscripts

William Griggs, Bernard Quaritch

Facsimiles of Illustrations in Biblical and Liturgical Manuscripts

ISBN/EAN: 9783744704274

Printed in Europe, USA, Canada, Australia, Japan

Cover: Foto ©ninafisch / pixelio.de

More available books at **www.hansebooks.com**

FACSIMILES

OF

ILLUSTRATIONS

IN

BIBLICAL AND LITURGICAL MANUSCRIPTS

executed in various countries

during the XI-XVI centuries
now in the possession of
BERNARD QUARITCH

With an introduction

LONDON
BERNARD QUARITCH
1892

Contents.

Order of arrangement.	Order as numbered.	Reference to number in Catalogue.		
1	170	12	Suabian Evangeliarium written about 1100: Miniature of St. Matthew.	Sec. XI
2	171		—— Miniature of St. Mark	
3	172		—— Miniature of St. John	
4	173	488	Ottenbeuern Collectarium, written about 1150: Miniature of God enthroned in majesty.	Sec. XII
5	174		—— Miniature of Assumption of the Virgin	
6	175		—— Miniature of St. Felix and his Brethren	
7	176		—— Miniature of Martyrdom of SS. Peter and Paul	
8	177	813	The Huntingfield Psalter, written in Norfolk or Lincolnshire about 1190: Two miniatures on one page	Sec. XII
9	178		—— Two Miniatures on one page	
10	179		—— Two Miniatures on one page	
11	180		—— Two Miniatures on one page	
12	181		—— Four Miniatures on one page	
13	182		Gifford Psalter, written in Suffolk about 1250: Initial Letter with ornamentation	Sec. XIII
14	183	260	The Clermont-Tonnerre Bible Historiale, written in France about 1370: God enthroned in majesty	Sec. XIV
15	184		—— Samson and Dalila	
16	185		—— History of Solomon: four miniatures on one page	
17	186		—— The Virgin and Child	
18	187	528	Livre d'Heures, written about 1370, perhaps at Meaux: Miniature of Christ bearing the Cross	Sec. XIV
19	188		—— Death and Coronation of the Virgin	
20	189	489	Proprium Sanctorum et Psalterium, written about 1400, probably for the use of Toulouse	Sec. XIV
21	190		—— the same	
22	191	460	Morosini Missal, written in Italy about 1420: The Crucifixion	Sec. XV
23	192		Lignage Livre d'Heures, written in France about 1420: Miniature of St. Catherine	Sec. XV
24	193	547	Livre d'Heures of Jacques de Bregilles, written in Flanders in 1442: The Annunciation	Sec. XV
25	194		—— Descent of the Holy Ghost	
26	195		—— Assumption of the Virgin	
27	206		Psalterium, written in England about 1450-60: Miniature in illustration of the 29th Psalm	Sec. XV
28	207		—— Miniature to the 31st Psalm	
29	196	548	Caumartin Livre d'Heures, written in Flanders about 1480: Martyrdom of St. Godeleve	Sec. XV
30	197		—— The Visitation	
31	198	554	Officium B. V. M., written about 1480-90, probably at Florence: Border and Miniature from the Vigils of the Dead	Sec. XV
32	199	534	The Condé Livre d'Heures, written about 1480-90 in France: The Annunciation, with smaller miniatures	Sec. XV
33	200		—— Saintly Queens of France	

Order of arrange- ment.	Order as numbered.	Reference to number in Catalogue.		
34	201	513	The Mount Olivet Psalter, written about 1490, probably at Siena: Page with border and miniatures	Sec. XV
35	202	823	Latin Primer, written in England by a Flemish artist about 1490: The Trinity	Sec. XV
36	203		———— St. Margaret	
37	204		———— St. Christopher	
38	205		———— St. Alban	
39	208	558	Psalterium or Prayerbook of Juana la Loca, written in Bruges about 1496, and illuminated by Gerart David: Miniature of St. Jerome, and an illuminated border	Sec. XV
40	209		———— Two pages with border and miniature. .	
41	210		———— St. Barbara, and a page with miniatured border .	
42	211		———— St. Christopher and a page with miniatured border	
43	212		———— A page with miniatured border .	
44	213	532	Livre d'Heures de Jouvenel des Ursins, written probably at Troyes about 1485: Miniature of St. Luke	Sec. XV
45	214	494	Breviarium of François de Castelnau, Archbishop of Narbonne (afterwards Cardinal de Clermont), written in 1501: Resurrection of Christ .	Sec. XVI
46	215		———— A page with miniatures and border	
47	216		Medici Psalterium, ascribed to Sinibaldo of Perugia, about 1505-10: Miniature and border . .	Sec. XVI

NOTE.

It will be observed that the only numeration on the following 47 plates begins with 170 and ends with 216. They are, however, properly numbered 1-47 in the list of contents. The former numbers relate to the order of their succession as portion of my series of "Choice examples selected from illuminated manuscripts, unpublished drawings, and illustrated books of early date." The total series is very various, and consists of—

Facsimiles of Bindings, 103 plates.
Miscellaneous Facsimiles, 8 plates.
The Comus Drawings of William Blake, 8 plates.
A Mexican MS., 31 plates.
Illustrations of Romances of Chivalry, 19 plates.
Illustrations of Liturgical and Biblical MSS., 47 plates.

Of the Miscellaneous Facsimiles, two plates (from the eighth century Purple Gospels) can be added to the present 47; and of the Romances of Chivalry, eight. The Illustrations from Biblical and Liturgical MSS. might thus be raised to the sum of 57 plates.

Introduction.

THE decoration of books with pictures and accessory ornament is a striking feature of medieval art. Some remnants of an earlier period, such as the fifth-century Virgil in the Laurentian library at Florence, show that the practice was not wholly new when it began its distinct career in the days of the Carolings. One may not unreasonably assume that the Helleno-Roman civilisation, which surrounded its domestic life with luxurious embellishments like the wall-paintings of Pompeii, would also have applied ornament to its books. If many examples of the kind had survived till the ninth century to furnish models for imitation by the Franco-Gauls, to whom we may ascribe the beginnings of medieval book-decoration, there would have been a better evidence of continuity in that art than we can allow to be discoverable. The style of design and the methods of ornamentation which are found in the books of the Middle Ages, present all the phases of birth, growth, and progressive development from the ninth century to the later part of the fifteenth. It is only at the close of this period that we find, in Italian books, something like a true revival of Helleno-Roman art, after a break of nearly a thousand years. It would consequently be improper to assert that medieval book-decoration arose in any phase of continuity from classical models.

An archetype is to some extent recognisable in Celtic and Celto-Saxon art, and also in manuscripts of Byzantine origin. It is customary now to regard Celtic art as a distant off-shoot from the Byzantine, among persons who forget that the Byzantine art which we know is not older than the Celtic, being itself entirely medieval. The appellation Byzantine conveys a false impression, since it leads to a confusion of two things identical only in name. The artistic qualities which are so called do not trace their origin to the Byzantium of Constantine, hardly perhaps to that of Justinian. It was Antioch and Alexandria—cities Greek by language, but Oriental by race, feeling, and taste—which contrived to supersede the Helleno-Roman art of old Byzantium or New Rome, and to set in its place that which we call Byzantine. Syria bestowed religion upon the Roman world, but only the eastern half of the empire, and the remote West, accepted her artistic teaching. The peculiar situation of Byzantium exposed it to the operation of new influences which Rome and Athens would have been less ready to undergo. As soon as paganism had faded away from Constantinople, there were no powerful traditions capable of retaining for any great length of time the Helleno-Roman art, which had been a mere transplantation from old Rome; and Christianity is responsible for the introduction of "Byzantine art" in books and pictures, with its stiff and conventional forms, its sombre and intense colours. It is also responsible for the creation of the similar modes of decorative art in the further lands of the west, which we find in the rude designs and gloomy colouring of Celtic manuscripts. The earliest missionaries and evangelisers, whose ardent zeal sustained them in bearing the torch to the ends of the world, were neither Greeks nor Latins, but men of Syrian or Egyptian blood, whose Hellenistic speech had furnished the language of the Septuagint and the Gospels. They were themselves of no high culture; their proselytes were usually confined to the lower classes of the people wherever they went, minds which needed pictorial aid for the realisation and the remembrance of the tale of faith. The teachers could give to their savage converts no other rudiments of art than were familiar to themselves; and even the Latin-speaking disciples who rose to aid and to succeed them, possessed no means of reforming a style of art which had become as sacred as its own symbolism. We can see evidences of this Eastern influence in the earliest pictorial efforts of Spain, Ireland, and Germany. The so-called Celtic, Visigothic or Germanic art is nothing more than that of Syria and Northern Egypt, filtered through successive generations of rude Christianised peoples. Hence the affinities which have been discovered between Byzantine and Celtic art, and again between Celtic and Saracenic methods of ornamentation.

Art in Italy was maintained at a higher level than elsewhere, notwithstanding the deteriorating influence of Gothic conquerors and Byzantine overlordship. Lombard and German invasions in the north, Arab and Norman aggressions in the south, all tended to delay its animation or revival. While elsewhere art grew from century to century in a natural process of development, called Gothic for want of a better name, the works of the Italian artists seem, for some centuries, to have been the result of a struggle against Gothicism on the one side, and Byzantinism on the other, with a small residuum of classical art as a basis. The success of the struggle became assured in the fourteenth century; the full and splendid renewal was made manifest in the fifteenth.

The story of Gaul was such that we need not consider whether its people had an art of their own. The Hellenism of Southern Gaul, the conquest by the Romans, the transmission of Helleno-Roman culture in the Provincia Romana, the conquest of the country by the Franks; and the initiation in the ninth century, among the Gallo-Franks, of the practice of illumination, which is our theme—form a complex picture, of which only the latest phase is necessary to be remarked.

As for Britain, when the Saxon immigration had become so great that the island was virtually Germanised, and as soon as the conquerors became aware that it was necessary to find a substitute for the civilisation they had destroyed, Irish art, such as it was, and Irish learning, which was somewhat better, were adopted and retained till the time of Henry Fitz-Empress. Then the decorative and pictorial art of France made itself a second home in England; and thenceforwards only local variety differentiated the art of the two countries during three centuries or more.

Works of German art are all subsequent in origin to the establishment of Karl the Great's empire, and in their earlier phases are identical, although ruder, with the achievements of Carolingian taste. They followed the same mode of development as the French school, always, however, exhibiting some national characteristics in the drawing of the human figure, and a crudeness in the colouring. Even when they had attained to extraordinary excellence in design at the beginning of the sixteenth century, their use of colours was still far inferior to that of their contemporaries.

Art in Spain in the middle ages, so far as we are concerned with it, was a successive adoption of French, Italian, and Flemish methods during the fourteenth and fifteenth centuries.

From the preceding remarks, it would appear unnecessary to trace mediæval book-decoration to any earlier origin than its own first revelations in the ninth and tenth centuries. The abortive efforts of Karl the Great to revive classical models were just enough to impregnate such traditions of Celtic and Germanic art as survived in Gaul, or had been imported from Ireland and England. The Art of Illumination was thus begotten, and made its home in central France.

The illuminated manuscripts of the ninth and tenth centuries are so few and so difficult of access, that there is no better way of studying them than in the plates of Count Bastard's work upon "L'Ornementation des Manuscrits." Those plates are exact and faithful, and, with a little supplementary aid from other sources, will supply all that is needed for the purpose. Ornamented manuscripts were not the rule but the exception until the thirteenth century. Pictorial designs and rudimentary borders appear sparsely in some books of the ninth, tenth, eleventh, and twelfth; but, to generalise roughly, it might be said that the age of miniatures began in the thirteenth century, and that of illuminated borders in the fourteenth. It was in the latter century also that illumination was first applied to profane literature, that is to chronicles, romances, and poetry.

The present collection of Facsimiles is restricted to biblical and liturgical books, which indeed retained their pre-eminent attractiveness for the illuminator even to the very end. It begins with three miniatures (Matthew, Mark, and John) from a Gospel-book written in Suabia, about the close of the eleventh century. The figures, on their ground of metallic gold, are undoubtedly imitated from some Byzantine type of the same age; but the tones of colour are lighter, and the border-ornamentation has a style of its own. One of the first things to strike the eye is the considerable quantity of green tints. That colour was much affected by the early illuminators and remained in favour with the Germans, the Dutch, and the Italians of Lombardy; but it fell into disuse among the French, the genuine Italians, and we may also say the English. Green is, in some sort, a criterion of antiquity: it may also be a token of the conservancy of primitive tastes. When green was employed by the skilled illuminators of the fourteenth and fifteenth centuries, it was so subordinated to the general scheme of colouring that it attracted no special notice. The Germans, however, always made considerable use of it; and the English occasionally indulged in green pigments with success. French artists rarely employed green in their miniatures; it appeared only in the foliage of their borders.

Plates 4, 5, 6, 7—from a book of Collects written in the Suabian monastery of Ottobeuern about the middle of the twelfth century—are of similar origin to the preceding three; but, so far as the figure-drawing is concerned, it is by no means an imitation of Byzantine work. Indeed, there is, in 4 and 5, a marked reminiscence of Celtic rudeness. On plate 6, the pseudo-classicism of the Frankish revival is seen in the group of martyrs at the top; in strong contrast with the thoroughly mediæval spirit expressed in the drawing of the monk below—apparently a portrait of the calligrapher presenting his work to "Alexander." This Alexander, who bore the same name as one of the saints in the group, was, perhaps, the patron for whom the book was written. In these paintings, the favourite green tint is not forgotten.

Plates 8—12 are from an English manuscript of unusually interesting character—a liturgical Psalter. There are several figures in each picture, and a certain dramatic energy appears in the compositions. The fine delineation of features—resembling pen-and-ink work—the long thin fingers of the personages, and the general tendency towards attenuation of extremities, indicate that the peculiar qualities of the art of the thirteenth century were now in their inception. The borders of the first four miniatures are more conventional and slighter than those of the German pictures (1, 2, 3), but there is a general resemblance. The dominant colours are blue and red; some tints of green may also be observed, but it is sparingly used, as the English or Anglo-Norman artist was now under the influence of the distinctly French school. The costumes and armour are those of the Normans and Angevins of Henry II's time, and some of the pictures have French inscriptions added as head-lines, but the artist was certainly an Englishman. The language of the inscriptions referred to is the Anglo-French of King John's time, and they were probably added some time after the completion of the manuscript. A few entries inserted in the Calendar in the fourteenth century show that the book must then have been in some East Anglian monastery connected with the house of Huntingfield; and the decidedly Yorkish character of the original calendar, taken in connection with that circumstance, is nearly sufficient evidence that the book was written in Lincolnshire or Norfolk. Plate 12 is one of some interesting additional designs which were added, evidently some years later than the others, but apparently by the same hand as executed all the rest. They differ in comprising four divisions to each miniature, instead of two. It is curious that the first of the four on plate 12 is the murder of Thomas à Beckett, an event which an English artist would probably have avoided limning before the close of the century in which it happened.

Plate 13 is a beautiful exercise in decoration. It is the large initial B of a Latin Psalter, the early English character of which is seen in the elegant and elaborate interlacements, adopted from Irish and Hiberno-Saxon methods of ornament, which fill the inner spaces of the great letter. Here we see, springing from the lower part of the initial, an extension which forms something like a partial border below. The lines run in curves broken by pointed projections, and bear, upon or close to them, some small grotesque figures. This is an early manifestation of the style which produced the ivy-leaf border, first by means of branching extensions from the letter, above and below, and the addition of gilt ivy-leaves at their extremities; finally, by making the border almost independent of the initial, and extending it so as to enclose the entire page, thus increasing the number of ivy-leaf patterns. The manuscript from which this plate is taken was probably written in Suffolk. The escutcheons painted in the upper right-hand margin are those of Gilbert de Clare, his wife Joan Plantagenet (Edward I's daughter), and John Earl of Warren—all three patrons of Clare Priory, to which the Countess Joan retired in her widowhood. They were painted about 1295, when the manuscript was, perhaps, some forty years old. The calendar is not of the York kind like that of the Huntingfield Psalter, but South-English in character.

Plates 14, 15, 16, 17, are taken from a manuscript of the celebrated version made by Guyart des Moulins in 1295, from the Historia Scholastica, or Bible History, of Peter Comestor. The manuscript was written not long after the middle of the fourteenth century; it is of purely French character, and is very beautiful. The drawing is much superior to that of the thirteenth century, although there is a considerable affinity in style. The figures are painted on elaborate artificial backgrounds, no longer on plain gold; and the effect of solidity or relief is obtained by a method of shading which was unknown in the preceding century. This is done by means of what is called cameo-work in a single colour (usually grey, grisaille), the gradations of tint being used with remarkable skill and delicacy for the modelling of the figures and the expression of the folds of drapery. A sprinkle of gold here and there, as in the addition of a crown on a helmet, was used to give light to the design. The elaborate back grounds become a noteworthy feature. They are chequered, or diapered, or laid out in the fashion of figured and embroidered tissues, giving a tone of rich completeness to the picture. The cameo or *camaieu* method remained a favourite one till the later part of the fifteenth century, but was not very frequently employed, because, though not showy, it required a rarer mastery than the handling of bright pigments. Plates 18, 19, are also in grisaille, from a little French prayerbook, written perhaps a few years later than the Bible. The work is not less clever, but it is a little rougher and less highly finished; and the ivy-leaf border, though it is now a complete frame to the page, is simpler and less elegant than it soon grew to be.

The latest and finest example of grisaille work is seen in plates 24, 25, 26. They are taken from a Livre d'Heures written in 1442 for Jacques de Bregilles, a Burgundian lord in the service of Duke Philippe le Bon. The book was illuminated on the occasion of his marriage; it has some pages of family records, and show that his usual residence was in Brussels. The Duke and Duchess, and the Countess of Charolois (wife of Charles the Bold) acted on various occasions as sponsors for the children of Jacques de Bregilles. The admirable quality of the paintings in his prayerbook is not adequately reproduced in the facsimiles. The artist must have been a man of consummate taste and skill. His borders are elegant; convolutions of branching and wreathing lines, as fine as if drawn with a pen, growing out into strawberries or flowers, or gold buds, with figures of birds here and there; and bits of conventional foliage in which gold and grisaille are delicately combined.

Plates 20, 21, are charming examples from a Toulouse Breviary, written, perhaps not so far south, about the year 1400. In their minute beauty and delicacy, they must be allowed to surpass everything else in the present collection. The manuscript is indeed a work of immaculate loveliness—the very perfection of French art—and the material on which it is written is the finest and thinnest of vellum.

Plate 22 introduces Italian art, in a Crucifixion from a missal supposed to have been illuminated for Cardinal Morosini about 1420. Harmony of colouring, effectiveness of composition, skilful treatment of draperies, are observable. There is, however, less of charm than of power in this dramatic tableau. A point of forcible contrast between it and the French works which precede and follow, is that while they look what they are—miniatures in a book, painted with more or less appearance of relief on a flat surface—the Italian Crucifixion seems to have rather the properties of a framed picture out of a gallery. This is caused partly by colouring, partly by a better sense of perspective.

Plate 23 is a St. Catherine, from a French Livre d'Heures, in which the rich chequered background of the miniature is contrasted with the light and elegant border formed of fine branching lines that bear gold buttons and ivy-leaves, and flowers coloured after nature. This style of border had already become a favourite one—about 1420-30—and was frequently used in France and England down to the latter part of the century. It was not till some forty or fifty years after the date of this manuscript that backgrounds began to be added to the borders as well as the miniatures.

Plates 27 and 28 are purely English work of a period not much later than the middle of the fifteenth century. They have for their miniatures diapered backgrounds such as have already been mentioned in connexion with the French Bible of 1370. Their borders are of the same style as in plate 23, but more elaborate and less elegant. The employment of green tints in the colouring is noticeable.

Plate 29, from a Franco-Flemish Livre d'Heures of about 1480, is not very dissimilar in style from the English pictures in 27, 28. It shows a narrow floral border of conventional type, painted on a background of gold, which is broadened on one side by a small outer border of the branch and flower type. The miniature is one of rare occurrence, representing the martyrdom of a local saint—St. Godeleve—in a green landscape, the town of Ghistele behind, and a curious fountain in the foreground. Plate 30 is from the same manuscript, and is more correct, but not less stiff in its drawing.

With the later decades of the fifteenth century, French and Flemish work affected solid architectural borders in gold, and a lavish use of that metal applied in a liquid form. The magnificence of the Burgundian court during the greater part of that century had attracted the best French artists, and their work and methods had resulted in raising the standard of Burgundo-Flemish art to such a height that the Flemish artists were now coming to the front and setting the fashion in ornament. The golden style we have mentioned is really a Flemish characteristic, but it was adopted everywhere. Plates 32 and 33 are French work of about 1490. In the former, the chief miniature is an Annunciation, which seems to be taking place in a private oratory, while the borders look like sections of a Gothic church, with niches and fretwork, and columns which yield compartments for smaller miniatures. Plate 33 is simpler, and shows four sainted queens of the Bourbon line; a fitting picture for the prayerbook from which the two plates are taken, since it was apparently executed for a member of the royal family. It belonged in the second half of the seventeenth century to the son of the great Condé.

The painting of floral designs on a border of pale liquid gold was probably of Flemish origin, but it was no less used in France than in Flanders at the same time as the architectural borders last spoken of. In France, however, it was not always completely followed; and we find in French manuscripts some effective composite borders, partly without a background, and partly on the liquid gold which is applied in bands taking the form of triangular or geometrical sections. The conventional ivy-leaves have disappeared; only a few of the natural flowers or fruits are represented, and the wreathed ornaments are thicker. An example is seen on plate 44, which is from a prayerbook executed at Troyes, about 1485, for a member of the family of Jouvenel des Ursins.

Plates 45 and 46 are from the Breviary of François de Castelnau, Archbishop of Narbonne (afterwards Cardinal de Clermont), a very gorgeous manuscript executed for him probably at Chateau-Gaillon near Rouen, in 1501. The borders are partly of the type of plates 32 and 33, partly of that of 44. It is a combination of the two Franco-Flemish styles. The ornamentation is extremely rich, and the designs are more plentiful than usual.

Plates 35-38 are fine examples of Flemish design, in a prayerbook executed in England, or for English use, towards the end of the fifteenth century. The figures are drawn and coloured in a manner which suggests rather the sixteenth, while the borders and backgrounds are rich and brilliant examples of the style of French work in the middle of the fifteenth century. Some of the borders are like an extension of the chequered background, others are singularly graceful specimens of the branches with ivy-leaves.

With the preceding plates, the Gothic school may be said to be left behind, except in so far as it formed an element in the work of the new Flemish school—the highest expression of Flemish art, such as we find it in plates 39-43. These are taken from a small Psalter or prayerbook, executed by Gherart David, probably at Bruges, in 1497. It is undoubtedly, from its style, age, and general appearance, one of a little group of books which the Archduke Philip, or his sister Margaret, commanded from that artist for presentation to members of the Spanish royal family, on account of the contemplated double nuptials. Of that little group of books, one is in the British Museum, two in the Imperial Library at Vienna, and one is perhaps in Brussels. This one was probably given by Philip to his wife, Juana la Loca, whom he married at Lille in 1496, and in whose right he became King-Consort of Castile in 1504. The Spanish character of the book appears in its calligraphy, and in the Castilian language of the Prayer of Saint Gregory. That it was intended for a lady is evinced by the word *peccadora* being used in that prayer as a translation of *peccator*. The beautiful borders in which flowers, apparently standing out in full relief from the tinted backgrounds, are painted with all the skill and accuracy of a student of nature; and the exquisite miniatures, some of which are *genre* pictures of marvellous grace and delicacy, seem to render these illustrations as completely distinct from mediæval art-work, as the Italian Renaissance-designs which appear in plates 31, 34, and 47.

Plate 31 is a page from a Florentine prayerbook written about 1480. The grim conception of the four diademed skulls, out of which spring the flowers and garlands that form a pretty, but somewhat heavy border, is intensified by the design within the initial, in which a shadowy skeleton with a scythe is reaping the harvest of Death in an atmosphere of ghostly dimness.

Plate 34 takes us to Siena. It is an exquisite page from a Psalter written for a patron or superior of the monks of St. Olivet. In the lovely Renaissance border on three of the sides are set little oval pictures—a Saviour, and a saint in steel armour. In the border at foot, an oblong space is occupied by a picture of the death of Goliath, with a charming landscape in the background. The beauty of the decorative design, the harmony of colours, the minute elegance of the little paintings, make this a delightful example of Italian art at the close of the fifteenth century.

Plate 47 is, like 34, a triumph of Italian art in the Renaissance. It is a page from a Psalter executed for a personage whose arms are a variation of those of the Florentine Medici. The central miniature and the eight little accessory pictures are of rare loveliness, and the borders, painted with gems and jewels, are ravishingly beautiful. Someone has ascribed the painting—done about 1505-10—to Sinibaldo of Perugia.

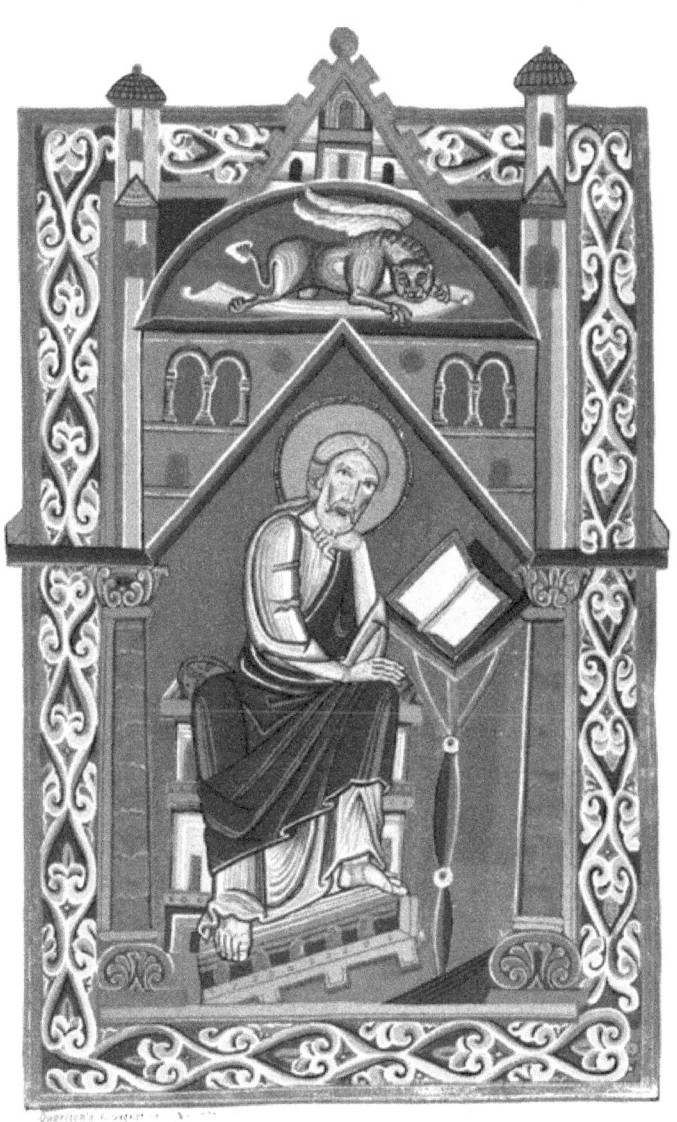

BOOK-ILLUMINATION: FACSIMILES FROM MSS.
Illustrations in Biblical and Liturgical MSS. down to the end of the Middle Ages.
Miniature of St. Mark.
From the Eichstett Evangeliarium, written about 1080.

BOOK-ILLUMINATION: FACSIMILES FROM MSS.
Illustrations in Biblical and Liturgical MSS. down to the end of the Middle Ages.
Miniature of St. Mark.
From the Eichstätt Evangeliarium, written about 1080.

BOOK-ILLUMINATION: FACSIMILES FROM MSS.

Illustrations in Biblical and Liturgical MSS. down to the end of the Middle Ages.

God in Majesty.

Miniature in the Ottenbeuern Collectaneum, written about 1160.

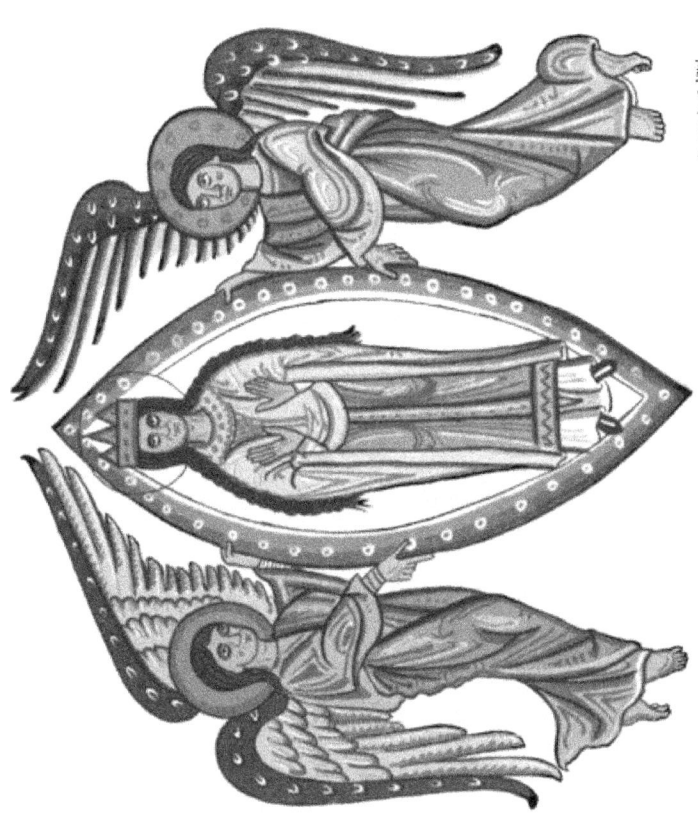

BOOK-ILLUMINATION: FACSIMILES FROM MSS.

Illustrations in Biblical and Liturgical MSS. down to the end of the Middle Ages.

The Assumption of the Virgin.

From the Missal in the Cathedral Library at Westminster.

BOOK-ILLUMINATION: FACSIMILES FROM MSS.
Illustrations in Biblical and Liturgical MSS. down to the end of the Middle Ages.
The Martyrs, St Felix and his Brothers.
From the Ottobeuren Collectaneum, written about 1160.

Evs·qui·ho
dierna oj · diem
apostoloru · tvoru.
Petri & Pavli martyrio
consecrasti, da ccclę tuę eoz
in omnibus sequi pceptum, pquos
religionis sumpsit exordium. Ro nde Syr.
Omps semp ds qui ecclam tuam in aplica

BOOK-ILLUMINATION: FACSIMILES FROM MSS.
Illustrations in Biblical and Liturgical MSS. down to the end of the Middle Ages.
Martyrdom of SS. Peter and Paul.
From the Ottobeuern Collectarium, written about 1160.

BOOK-ILLUMINATION: FACSIMILES FROM MSS.

Illustrations in Biblical and Liturgical MSS. down to the end of the Middle Ages.
Building of towers; Abraham's battle with four kings.
From the Huntingfield Psalter, written about 1180-90.

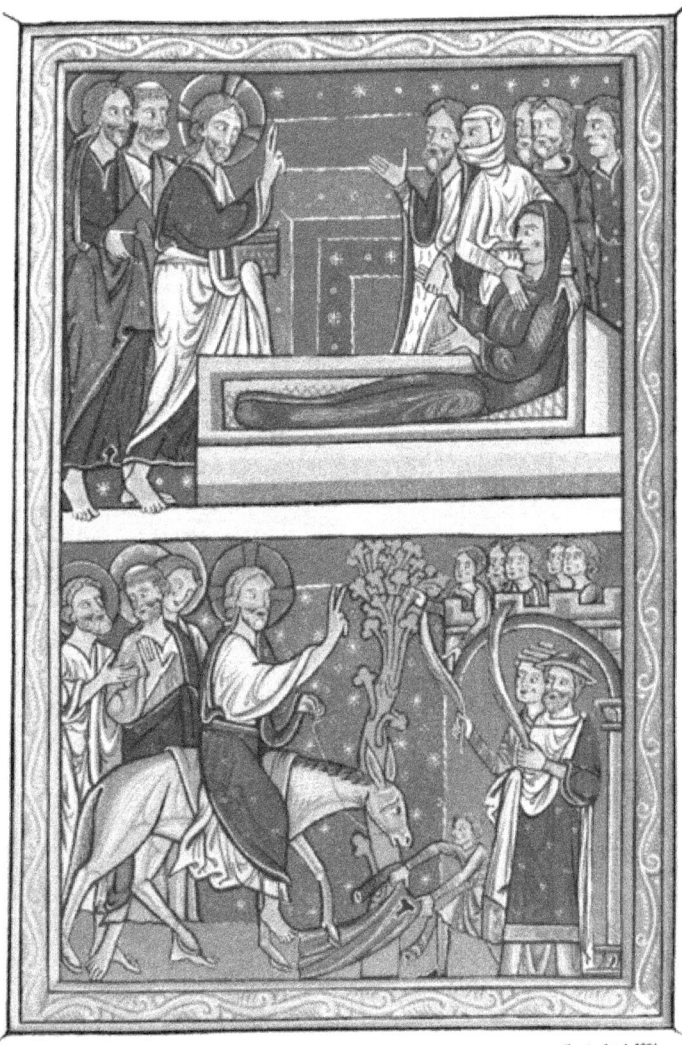

BOOK-ILLUMINATION: FACSIMILES FROM MSS.

Illustrations in Biblical and Liturgical MSS. down to the end of the Middle Ages

Christ healing Peter's mother-in-law; Christ's Entry into Jerusalem.
From the Huntingfield Psalter, written about 1180-90.

BOOK-ILLUMINATION: FACSIMILES FROM MSS.

Illustrations in Biblical and Liturgical MSS. down to the end of the Middle Ages

*Four Scenes of Martyrdom; including the Slaying of St. Thomas Becket.
From the Huntingfield Psalter, written about 1300 (?).*

BOOK-ILLUMINATION: FACSIMILES FROM MSS.

Illustrations in Biblical and Liturgical MSS. down to the end of the Middle Ages.

Initial Letter from the Gifford Psalter, written at Clare Priory about 1250; having the arms of Gilbert de Clare and Joan of Acre added on the margins.

BOOK-ILLUMINATION: FACSIMILES FROM MSS.
Illustrations in Biblical and Liturgical MSS. down to the end of the Middle Ages.
Delilah's Treachery to Samson.
From the Clermont-Tonnerre Bible Historiaux, written about 1370.

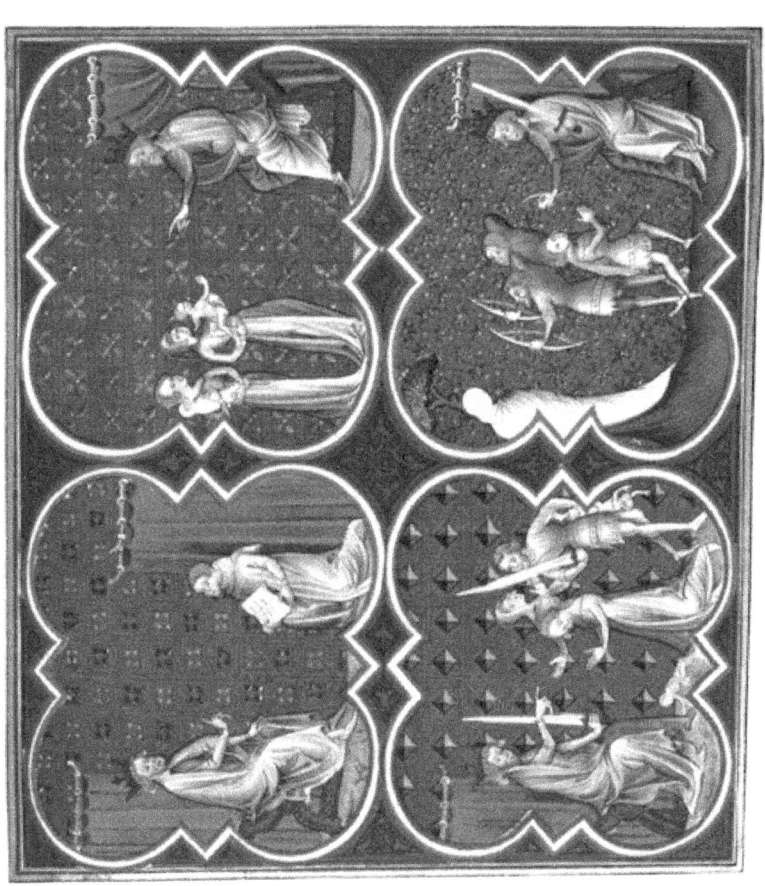

BOOK-ILLUMINATION: FACSIMILES FROM MSS.
Illustrations in Biblical and Liturgical MSS. down to the end of the Middle Ages.
The Code of Solomon.
From the Chronik-Tapisserie Bible, written about 1370.

BOOK-ILLUMINATION: FACSIMILES FROM MSS.
Illustrations in Biblical and Liturgical MSS. down to the end of the Middle Ages.
The Virgin and Child
From the Clermont-Tonnerre Bible, written about 1370

ILLUSTRATIONS IN RELIGIOUS BOOKS TOWARDS THE END OF THE MIDDLE AGES.
Miniature of Christ bearing the Cross.
From the Hours, Latin and French, of Charles V., about 1364.

BOOK-ILLUMINATION: FACSIMILES FROM MSS.
Illustrative of Biblical and Liturgical MSS. down to the end of the Middle Ages.
Death and Coronation of the Virgin.
From the Hours Livre d'Heures, written in France about 1470.

BOOK-ILLUMINATION: FACSIMILES FROM MSS.
Illustrations in Biblical and Liturgical MSS. down to the end of the Middle Ages.
A page from the Calendar of a Breviary written in Southern France about the year 1400.

BOOK-ILLUMINATION: FACSIMILES FROM MSS.

Illustrations in Biblical and Liturgical MSS. down to the end of the Middle Ages.

A page, with a miniature of St. George, from a Breviary written in Southern France about the year 1480.

BOOK-ILLUMINATION: FACSIMILES FROM MSS.

*Illustrations in Biblical and Liturgical MSS. down to the end of the Middle Ages.
The Crucifixion.
From the Morisini Missal, written in Italy about 1420.*

BOOK-ILLUMINATION: FACSIMILES FROM MSS.
Illustrations in Biblical and Liturgical MSS. down to the end of the Middle Ages.
Miniature of St. Katherine.
From the Lignaye Heures, written in Central France about 1420.

BOOK-ILLUMINATION: FACSIMILES FROM MSS.
Illustrations in Biblical and Liturgical MSS. down to the end of the Middle Ages.

A page from the Heures de Jacques de Brégilles,
executed (at Brussels?) in 1412.

BOOK-ILLUMINATION: FACSIMILES FROM MSS.
Illustrations in Biblical and Liturgical MSS. down to the end of the Middle Ages.

A page from the Heures de Jacques de Brégilles,
executed (at Brussels?) in 1412.

BOOK-ILLUMINATION: FACSIMILES FROM MSS.
Illustrations in Liturgical and Liturgical MSS. down to the end of the Middle Ages
Miniature in illustration of the 81st Psalm.
From a Psalterium of English work, written about 1450.

BOOK-ILLUMINATION: FACSIMILES FROM MSS.

Illustrations in Biblical and Liturgical MSS. down to the end of the Middle Ages

Martyrdom of St. Godeleve

From the Caumartin Hours, written in Artois about 1500

BOOK-ILLUMINATION: FACSIMILES FROM MSS.
Illustrations in Biblical and Liturgical MSS. down to the end of the Middle Ages.
The Visitation: The Virgin Mary and St. Elizabeth.
From the Carmarthen Horæ, written in Artois about 1480.

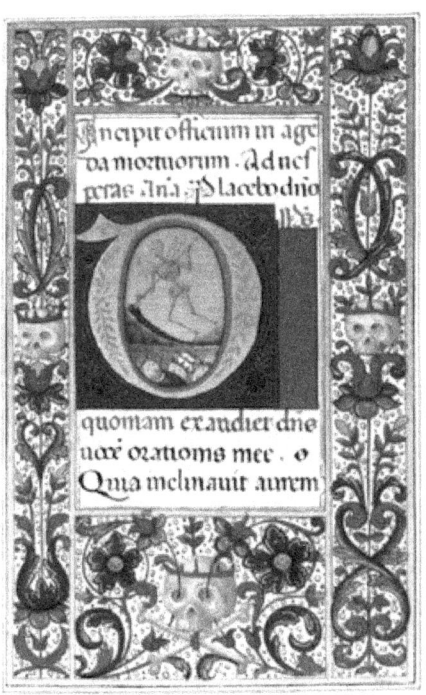

BOOK-ILLUMINATION: FACSIMILES FROM MSS.
Illustrations in Biblical and Liturgical MSS. down to the end of the Middle Ages.
Page with initial, miniature and border.
From the Officium B.V.M., an Italian MS. written about 1480.

BOOK-ILLUMINATION: FACSIMILES FROM MSS.
Illustrations in Liturgical and Liturgical MSS. down to the end of the Middle Ages
Miniature of the Annunciation.
From the Cat. de Livre d'Heures, written in France about 1490.

BOOK-ILLUMINATION: FACSIMILES FROM MSS.

Illustrations in Liturgical and Liturgical MSS. down to the end of the Middle Ages

Saint of Ladies of the House of Bourbon

From the Livre d'Heures, written in France about 1480.

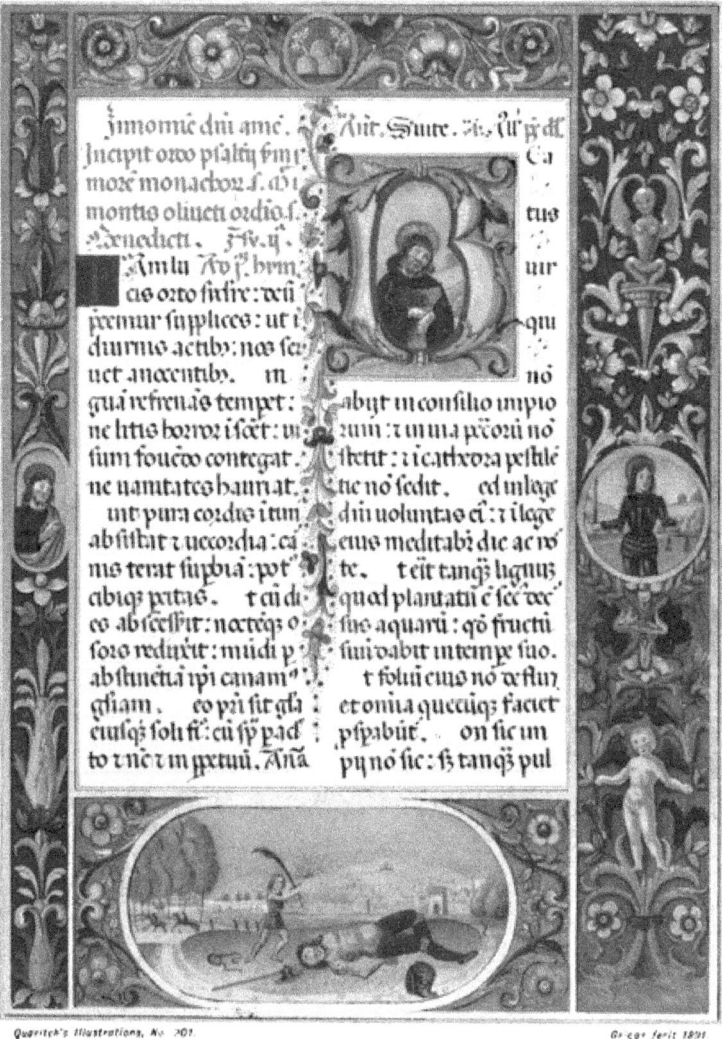

BOOK-ILLUMINATION: FACSIMILES FROM MSS.
Illustrations in Biblical and Liturgical MSS. down to the end of the Middle Ages.

BOOK-ILLUMINATION: FACSIMILES FROM MSS.
Illustrations in Biblical and Liturgical MSS. down to the end of the Middle Ages.
The Trinity
From a Latin Primer written in England by a Flemish hand about 1490.

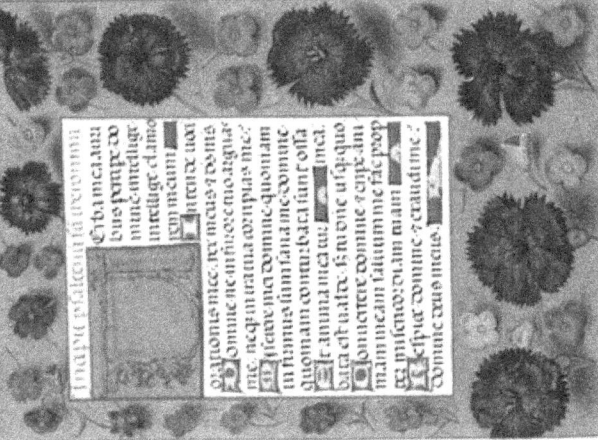
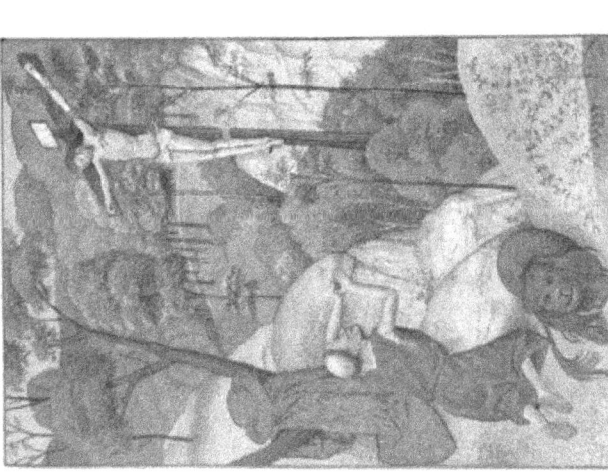

BOOK-ILLUMINATION: FACSIMILES FROM MSS.

Illustrations in Biblical and Liturgical MSS. down to the end of the Middle Ages.

Miniature of St. Jerome, and a page with border

From the Prayer-Book of Juana of Castile, illuminated by Gherart Davit of Bruges, about 1498.

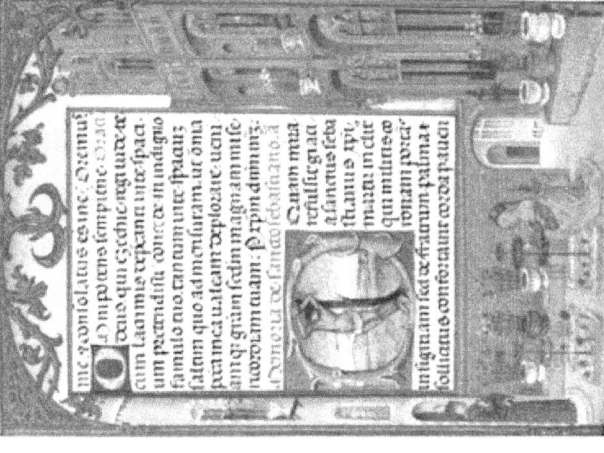

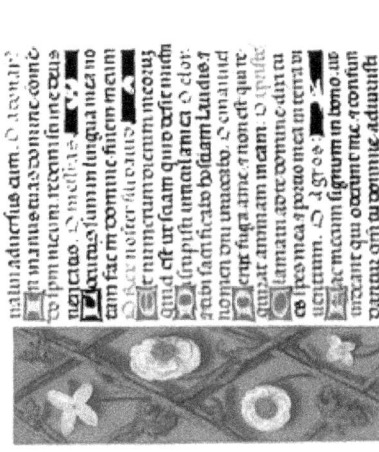

BOOK-ILLUMINATION: FACSIMILES FROM MSS.

Illustrations in Biblical and Liturgical MSS. down to the end of the Middle Ages.

Two pages: Miniature and borders.

From the Prayer-Book of Juana of Castile, illuminated by Gheraert Davit of Bruges, about 1498.

BOOK-ILLUMINATION: FACSIMILES FROM MSS.

Illustrations in Biblical and Liturgical MSS. down to the end of the Middle Ages.

Miniature of St. Barbara, and border with figures.

From the Prayer-Book of Joanna of Castile, illuminated by Gherart David of Bruges, about 1498.

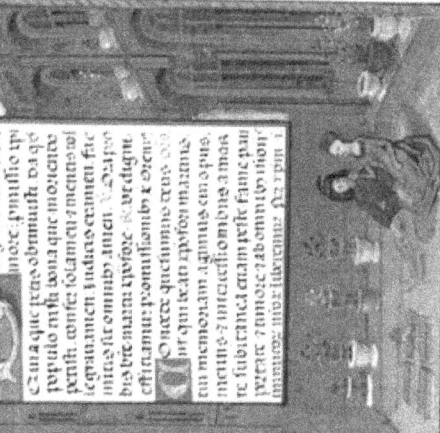

BOOK-ILLUMINATION: FACSIMILES FROM MSS.

Illustrations in Biblical and Liturgical MSS. down to the end of the Middle Ages.

Miniature of St. Christopher, and a page with border.

From the Prayer-Book of Joanna of Castile, illuminated by Gheraert Horrid of Bruges, about 1500.

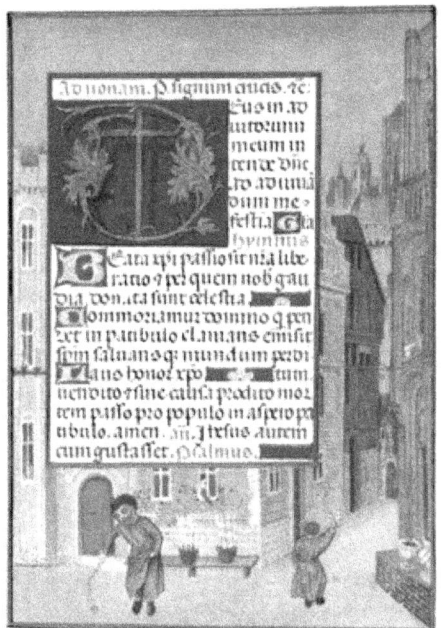

BOOK-ILLUMINATION: FACSIMILES FROM MSS.

Illustrations in Biblical and Liturgical MSS. down to the end of the Middle Ages.

A page-border with Miniature.

From the Prayer-Book of Juana of Castile,
illuminated by Gherart David of Bruges, about 1498.

BOOK-ILLUMINATION: FACSIMILES FROM MSS.
Illustrations in Biblical and Liturgical MSS. down to the end of the Middle Ages
Picture of St. Luke.
From a Livre d'Heures, written at Bourges in 1905 for Jouvenel des Ursins.

BOOK-ILLUMINATION: FACSIMILES FROM MSS.

Illustrations in Biblical and Liturgical MSS. down to the end of the Middle Ages

Miniature of the Resurrection of Christ.

From the Castelnau Breviary, written for the Cardinal de Clermont in 1501.

BOOK-ILLUMINATION: FACSIMILES FROM MSS.
Illustrations in Biblical and Liturgical MSS. down to the end of the Middle Ages.
A Page with small Miniatures.
From the Castelnau Breviary, written for the Cardinal de Clermont in 1501.

BOOK-ILLUMINATION: FACSIMILES FROM MSS.

Illustrations in Biblical and Liturgical MSS. down to the end of the Middle Ages.

First page of a Psalter executed apparently for one of the Medici family;
attributed to Sinibaldo of Perugia (about 1505).

www.ingramcontent.com/pod-product-compliance
Lightning Source LLC
Chambersburg PA
CBHW032244080426
42735CB00008B/989